# A Gathering of Honey

To Alexander, whose head is full of quotations

# A Gathering of Honey

HERMIONE MONCREIFFE

THE CHOIR PRESS

First published in the United Kingdom in 2019 by
The Choir Press

ISBN 978-1-78963-055-8

# *Foreword*

So often there is a lack of purpose and point in the lives of many.

So often people are inspired by the lives and achievements and purposes of others.

In all things there is a need for motivation and engagement in life as well as inspiration.

This book is an attempt to find some of those quotations and words and sentiments that mean much to and have inspired people who are in the public eye or, less overtly, who have been successful whether privately or publicly.

It is, as it were, a handing on of wisdom and an attempt to share and encourage others to live fulfilled and fulfilling lives. It covers spiritual as well as physical and mental propositions.

Antony Sutch

# *Acknowledgements*

First of all, Antony Sutch. The idea for this book was his. Tremendous thanks to him not only for the idea,but also for his constant encouragement and enthusiasm. Also much gratitude to Julia Rood and Lucy Warhurst for their technical skills. Then of course, so many thanks to everyone at The Choir Press, who were ever efficient and friendly.

Finally, there would have been no book at all, if it was not for the great generosity of the people who answered my letters or emails with their wonderful contributions.

# *Preface*

The contributors of this book were usually people I knew, friends of friends or those with whom I had some other link. I wrote to them saying that I was editing a book of quotations from mystics, saints, gurus, philosophers, poets and the wise, asking if they could send me any such which meant something to them in their life and activity.

Hermione Moncreiffe

# His Holiness the Dalai Lama

*Given by His Holiness's private secretary Tenzin Taklha.*

**The last of the three verses below has always been an inspiration for His Holiness the Dalai Lama:**

For those who admire the spiritual ideals of the Eight verses on Transforming the Mind it is helpful to recite the following verses for generating the mind for enlightenment. Practicing Buddhists should recite the verses and reflect upon the meaning of the words, while trying to enhance their altruism and compassion. Those of you who are practitioners of other religious traditions can draw from your own spiritual teachings, and try to commit yourselves to cultivating altruistic thoughts in pursuit of the altruistic ideal.

> **With a wish to free all beings**
> **I shall always go for refuge**
> **to the Buddha, Dharma and Sangha**
> **until I reach full enlightenment.**
>
> **Enthused by wisdom and compassion,**
> **today in the Buddha's presence**
> **I generate the Mind for Full Awakening**
> **for the benefit of all sentient beings.**
>
> **As long as space endures,**
> **as long as sentient beings remain,**
> **until then, may I too remain**
> **and dispel the miseries of the world.**

In conclusion, those who like myself, consider themselves to be followers of Buddha, should practice as much as we can. To followers of other religious traditions, I would like to say, 'Please practice your own religion seriously and sincerely.' And to non-believers, I request you to try to be warm-hearted. I ask this of you because these mental attitudes actually bring us happiness. As I have mentioned before, taking care of others actually benefits you.

'Generating the Mind for Enlightenment',
The Office of His Holiness the Dalai Lama

## Rosanna Gardner, artist

One saying I like is a Chinese proverb:

**Keep a green bough within your heart and the singing birds will come.**

I also like Hilaire Belloc:

**From quiet homes and first beginning**
**Out to the undiscovered ends,**
**There's nothing worth the wear of winning**
**But laughter and the love of friends**

Hilaire Belloc (1870–1953)

————◄○►————

## Tom Stoppard, playwright

**Life must be lived as a contest of generosity.**

Unfortunately I don't know who said it or wrote it, but he or she was certainly a 'guru' of some kind.

## Ciara Connell, humanitarian aid worker, co-founder of refugee women's centre, self defence instructor

**It is only with the heart that one can see rightly; what is essential is invisible to the eye.**

The Little Prince (London: Egmont, 2017),<br>Antoine de Saint-Exupéry (1900–1944), translated by Katherine Woods

———◄o►———

## Libby Purves, radio presenter, journalist and author

One which my mother constantly quoted – I have no idea who from – was this; it starts pious and then deflates itself:

**God put us here on earth to help others. What he put the others here for ... God only knows!**

# Judi Dench, actor

A very dear friend of ours, Herman Barr, once said to me:

**Always look for the plusses.**

I have never forgotten it and it has become a watchword in our family.

————◄o►————

# Sophie van den Bogaerde, Concert Pianist

A friend took me out to lunch a while ago and told me she'd earned a lot of money that year, all from selling her paintings. I asked her how she'd managed to achieve such a feat and she said, 'I just put my mind to it.' This is what I think of when in need of motivation and reminds me of this poem by Goethe:

> **Lose this day loitering – 'twill be the same story**
> **To-morrow – and the next more dilatory;**
> **Then indecision brings its own delays,**
> **And days are lost lamenting o'er lost days.**
> **Are you in earnest? seize this very minute –**
> **What you can do, or dream you can, begin it,**
> **Boldness has genius, power, and magic in it,**
> **Only engage, and then the mind grows heated –**
> **Begin it, and the work will be completed!**

*Faust* (1835), Johann Wolfgang von Goethe (1749–1832),
translated by John Anster

*Julian Fellowes, actor, novelist, film director and screenwriter, and a Conservative peer of the House of Lords*

I do have certain phrases and maxims I live by, although I am not convinced they are weighty enough for your purposes. One of my favourites was my grandmother's advice:

**Never make an enemy by accident.**

She had, of course, no objection to making one on purpose. I agree with my stepmother's adage:

**Never let anyone be rude to you twice. The second time is your fault.**

Which I must say she stuck to.

I like Cecil Rhodes's observation to Lord Grey:

**You are an Englishman, and have consequently drawn the greatest prize in the lottery of life,**

Cecil Rhodes (1853–1902)

which I endorse.

On a slightly different plane, I have always been moved by the response of the young Marie Antoinette (1755–1793) when she was taken to Paris for the first time, in 1773. The crowds surrounded the Hotel de Ville, shrieking their enthusiastic support, and the Baron de Breteuil, who had accompanied her, observed, 'See. See how the people love you.' To which the seventeen-year-old Dauphine replied, 'Yes. But what if they should hate you?'

Finally, I would suggest Noël Coward's words:

**Work is more fun than fun.**

Noël Coward (1899–1973)

This seems to me a fairly crucial component of a successful life. One, that there must be work of some kind, and, two, that it must absorb and fulfil you. I believe that.

## Ysenda Maxtone Graham, author, book reviewer and columnist

I always love this one from my grandmother Jan Struther's *Mrs Miniver* – a thought that came to her when she looked into her car's rear-view mirror:

**You cannot successfully navigate the future unless you keep always framed beside it a small, clear image of the past.**

*Mrs Miniver* (London: Virago, 1989), Jan Struther (1901–1953)

## *Jon Connell, founder of* The Week *magazine*

Among those whom I like or admire, I can find no common denominator, but among those whom I love, I can: all of them make me laugh.

W H Auden (1907–1973)

The heights that great men reached and kept
were not attained by sudden flight,
But they, while their companions slept, toiled
ever upward through the night.

Henry Wadsworth Longfellow (1807–1882)

As I went out into the world, I would meet two sorts of great men: there were the little great men, who made all those around them feel little, and the great great men, who made all those around them feel great.

G K Chesterton (1874–1936)

Enough, if something from our hands have power
To live, and act, and serve the future hour;
And if, as toward the silent tomb we go,
Through love, through hope, and faith's
transcendent dower,
We feel that we are greater than we know.

'After-Thought', William Wordsworth (1770–1850)

## Joanna Lumley, actress, author and activist

May I offer from Rabindranath Tagore ... I love it and hope it is suitable:

**Death is not extinguishing the light: it is only putting out the lamp because the dawn has come.**

Rabindranath Tagore (1861–1941)

JOANNA LUMLEY

Dear Lady Moncreiffe,
Thank you so much for your letter: what a wonderful book you are making.
May I offer, from Rabindranath Tagore:
" Death is not extinguishing the light: it is only putting out the lamp because the dawn has come."
I love it, and hope it is suitable..
with a thousand good wishes and much admiration
yours sincerely, Joanna Lumley ← pen playing up....

## Joe Gibbs, founder of the Belladrum Tartan Heart Festival

I would choose '*Solvitur ambulando*' – loosely translated as 'work it out by walking'.

———◄○►———

## Brother Columbarnus-Mary, hermit

*Chosen for him by Joe Gibbs.*

**Silentium est aureum.**

Latin for 'Silence is golden'

———◄○►———

## Peter Roper-Curzon, concert pianist, composer and organist

**However difficult life may seem, there is always something you can do and succeed at.**

Stephen Hawking (1942–2018)

## Victoria Roper-Curzon, founder of Elfie London Childrenswear

**Carpe diem.**

Latin for 'Seize the day'

———◁○▷———

## Mary Stewart, yoga teacher, artist

**We are each a unique incarnation of God's love.**

Peter Broadhurst, servite monk, died 2007

**Any religion can be a vehicle between God and man, just as any religion can deteriorate into magical or commercial practices, to be turned into an instrument for tormenting one's fellow men.**

Fosco Maraini (1912–2004)

**It is better to sit down in a modest ignorance and rest content with the natural blessing of our own reasons, than buy the uncertain knowledge of this life with sweat and vexation, which death gives every fool gratis.**

Sir Thomas Browne (1605–1682)

## Piers Jackson, artist

I'm a huge fan of Socrates. I love this one from *Phaedo*:

> Philosophy provides the soul with a calm retreat.
> By following and being always engaged in reason,
> the philosopher's soul keeps its eyes on what is
> true, divine, and not the object of opinion.

*Phaedo*, Socrates (c. 470–399 BC)

————◀◉▶————

## Siobhan Dundee, chatelain

> The true work of art is but a shadow of the divine
> perception. Only God creates. The rest of us just
> copy.

Michelangelo (1475–1564)

## Linda Kelly, author, historian

**No act of kindness, however small, is ever in vain.**

'The Lion and the Mouse', Aesop (c. 620–564 BC)

———◄○►———

## Alexandra Moncreiffe, nutritionist, health coach, model

**Take your practiced powers and stretch them out until they span the chasm between two contradictions
For the god wants to know himself in you.**

'As Once the Winged Energy of Delight', Rainer Maria Rilke
(1875–1926)

**People may say bad things about you, but you should never say bad things about yourself.**

*The Love Guru* (2008), Mike Myers (born 1963)

# William Lovelady, composer, guitarist

Here are some extracts from the Chinese philosopher Lao Tzu, who happens to be a favourite of mine:

> **The journey of a thousand miles begins with one step.**
>
> Lao Tzu (born 601 BC)

> **Those who know do not speak. Those who speak do not know.**
>
> Lao Tzu (born 601 BC)

> **Care what other people think and you will always be their prisoner.**
>
> Lao Tzu (born 601 BC)

## *Serena Fass, author*

By FAR my favourite quote, which I have by my bed and look at most mornings, is something sent to me by Mother Teresa, now St Teresa of Calcutta, which says:

> **God has not called me to be successful. He has called me to be faithful.**

St Teresa of Calcutta (1910–1977)

It is a very good verse against pride.

## *Nell Gifford, founder of Giffords Circus*

Marriage is in many ways a simplification of life, and it naturally combines the strengths and wills of two young people so that, together, they seem to reach farther into the future than they did before. Above all, marriage is a new task and a new seriousness – a new demand on the strength and generosity of each partner, and a great new danger for both.

The point of marriage is not to create a quick commonality by tearing down all boundaries; on the contrary, a good marriage is one in which each partner appoints the other to be the guardian of their solitude, and thus they show each other the greatest possible trust.

A merging of two people is an impossibility, and where it seems to exist, it is a hemming-in, a mutual consent that robs one party or both parties of their fullest freedom and development. But once the realisation is accepted that even between the closest people infinite distances exist, a marvellous living side by side can grow up for them, if they succeed in loving the expanse between them, which gives them the possibility of always seeing each other as a whole and before an immense sky.

... for the more we are, the richer everything we experience is. And those who want to have a deep love in their lives must collect and save for it and gather honey.

*Letters to a Young Poet* (Read, 2007), Rainer Maria Rilke (1875–1926),
translated by Jane Bannard Greene

## Alice Macdonald, artist

The quote I have decided on is one that my friend told me when I was stuck on a painting, but it was originally said by Grayson Perry (born 1960). He says that when trying to make art it is important to

**Take all your musings seriously.**

I can't find the right quote, but I think he also said something like:

**You should be kind to your ideas and nurture them as you never know where they will lead to.**

I have found it to be very useful advice and I often have it in mind when I am in my studio and wondering what to do, or when there is something I am considering doing but I'm not sure about it.

————◄○►————

## Ivar Wigan, photographer

**Darkness cannot drive out darkness; only light can do that. Hate cannot drive out hate; only love can do that.**

Martin Luther King (1929–1968)

## Tom Stacey, author

**You never enjoy the world aright, till the Sea itself floweth in your veins, till you are clothed with the heavens, and crowned with the stars ...**

*Centuries of Meditations* (Shrine of Wisdom, 2002),
Thomas Traherne (c. 1636–1674)

This quote impelled me to write *A Dark and Stormy Night.*

———◄o►———

## Jacob Rees-Mogg, Member of Parliament

The most suitable quotation I can think of is the famous one attributed to St Julian of Norwich:

**All shall be well, and all shall be well and all manner of thing shall be well.**

St Julian of Norwich (c. 1342–1416)

## Rachel Kelly, author and mental health advocate

How about:

**My strength is made perfect in weakness.**

St Paul, 2 Corinthians 12:9

————◄◦►————

## John Julius Norwich, author

May I suggest that admirable maxim by Cambridge philosopher C D Broad?

**A healthy appetite for righteousness, kept in due control by good manners, is an excellent thing; but to 'hunger and thirst' after it is often merely a symptom of spiritual diabetes.**

C D Broad (1887–1971)

## Leonie Gibbs, painter and sculptor

From a family motto:

Be of a tranquil mind.

———◄○►———

## David Roper-Curzon, sculptor

*Spes deus.*

Family motto. Latin for 'My hope is in God'

———◄○►———

## Peregrine Moncreiffe, investment trader

The word 'good' has many meanings. For example, if a man were to shoot his grandmother at a range of five hundred yards, I should call him a good shot, but not necessarily a good man.

G K Chesterton (1874–1936)

To love means loving the unlovable. To forgive means pardoning the unpardonable. Faith means believing in the unbelievable. Hope means hoping when everything seems hopeless.

G K Chesterton (1874–1936)

## Mervyn Fox-Pitt, founder of polo in Scotland

**Put peace into each other's hand and like a treasure hold it.
Protect it like a candle flame, with tenderness enfold it ...**

Hymn, Fred Kaan (1929–2009)

————◄○►————

## Simon Tarrant, artist and curator

The following quote has great meaning for me.

**Life is short, art long, opportunity fleeting, experience treacherous, judgement difficult.**

Hippocrates (c. 460–370 BC)

## Leanda de Lisle, biographer

The quotation I would like to offer is from Demosthenes.

**Nothing is easier than self-deceit. For what every man wishes, that he also believes to be true.**

Demosthenes (384–322 BC)

————◄O►————

## Emma Murphy, painter

**He who awaits much can expect little.**

Gabriel García Márquez (1927–2014)

**Even when the winds of misfortune blow, amazing things can still happen.**

Gabriel García Márquez (1927–2014)

**Don't struggle so much; the best things happen when not expected.**

Gabriel García Márquez (1927–2014)

## Tom Faulkner, furniture maker and creative director

This is one I like:

> Patience is the calm acceptance that things can happen in a different order than the one you have in mind.

David G Allen

———◄o►———

## Flora Connell, musician

This Picasso quotation holds particular meaning for me.

> Art washes away from the soul the dust of everyday life.

Pablo Picasso (1881–1973)

# Philip Thompson, founder of Waddler Clothing

Below are two quotes that I love.

> We dream the flight but we fear the height. To fly one needs to have the courage to face the void. The flight can only happen in the void. The void is the space for freedom, the absence of certainties. But that is what we fear: not having certainties. That is why we change the flight for cages. Cages are the place where certainties live.
>
> The Brothers Karamazov (1880), Fyodor Dostoyevsky (1821–1881)

> If you begin to understand what you are without trying to change it, then what you are undergoes a transformation.
>
> Jiddu Krishnamurti (1895–1986)

# Alexander Dundee, Council of Europe parliamentarian and UK consul for Croatia in Scotland

A pessimist sees the difficulty in every opportunity; an optimist sees the opportunity in every difficulty.

Winston Churchill (1874–1965)

Moonlight floods the whole sky from horizon to horizon; how much it can fill your room depends on its windows.

Jalal ad-Din Muhammad Rumi (1207–1273)

———◄○►———

# B H Fraser

Have a good conscience and thou shalt ever have joy. A good conscience is able to bear very much, and is very cheerful in adversities.

St Thomas Aquinas (1225–1274)

You are your only master.
Who else?
Subdue yourself
And discover your master.

The Buddha (fifth/sixth century BC, exact dates unknown)

# Edward Cazalet, craniosacral therapist

Tao is beyond words
And beyond things.
It is not expressed
Either in word or in silence.
Where there is no longer word or silence
Tao is apprehended.

*The Way of Chuang Tzu* (New York, NY: New Directions, 1969),
translated by Thomas Merton

The purpose of words is to convey ideas. When the ideas are grasped, the words are forgotten.

Where can I find a man who has forgotten words? He is the one I would like to talk to.

*The Way of Chuang Tzu*, translated by Thomas Merton

# Alan Rush, researcher, Middle East dynasties

*Omnia mirari etiam tritissima.*

Carl Linnaeus, Swedish botanist, zoologist, physician (1707–1778).
Latin for 'Find wonder in all things, even the most commonplace'

This being human is a guest house.
Every morning a new arrival.

A joy, a depression, a meanness,
some momentary awareness comes
as an unexpected visitor.

Welcome and entertain them all!
Even if they're a crowd of sorrows,
who violently sweep your house
empty of its furniture,
still, treat each guest honourably.
He may be clearing you out
for some new delight.

The dark thought, the shame, the malice,
meet them at the door laughing,
and invite them in.

Be grateful for whoever comes,
because each has been sent
as a guide from beyond.

Jalal ad-Din Muhammad Rumi (1207–1273)

## Ninian Crichton Stuart, hereditary keeper of Falkland Palace

Sent to you from my own hut in the forest of Falkland. I am trying to live as a dedicated steward of the stone, wood and waters of life and of land. So a trilogy of quotations:

**Stone is the tabernacle of memory.**

John O'Donohue (1956–2008)

**I went to the woods because I wished to live deliberately, to front only the essential facts of life, and see if I could not learn what it had to teach, and not, when I came to die, discover that I had not lived.**

Henry David Thoreau (1817–1862)

**I would love to live like a river flows, carried by the surprise of its own unfolding.**

John O'Donohue (1956–2008)

# Ossian Moncreiffe, composer

**Where words fail, music speaks.**

Hans Christian Andersen (1805–1875)

**Without music, life would be a mistake.**

Friedrich Nietzsche (1844–1900)

## Minnie Murphy, actor

I have two favourite quotes. One is Pushkin:

> **Whatever happens to me, be sure that my last thought and last prayer shall be for you.**

Alexander Pushkin (1799–1837)

The other is Thomas More:

> **Pray for me, as I will for thee, that we will merrily meet in heaven.**

Thomas More (1478–1535)

# Fiona Hodgson, politician and life peer

**Life isn't about waiting for the storm to pass; it's about learning to dance in the rain.**

Vivian Greene (1904–2003)

———◄o►———

# Hermione Moncreiffe, author

I think often of the words of Father Agathon of the fifth century. Whenever his instinct was to pass judgement on something, he would say to himself, *'Agathon, it isn't your business to do that.'*

# Louisa Thomas, solicitor

Here are some of my favourites.

> **'What is the odds so long as the fire of soul is kindled at the taper of conwiviality *(sic)*, and the wing of friendship never moults a feather!'**
>
> *The Old Curiosity Shop* (Ware: Wordsworth, 1995),
> Charles Dickens (1812–1870)

This was a favourite quote of my parents' greatest friends and we toasted the 'wing of friendship' every year we visited them in Hampshire from Lancashire. My brother and I carry on the tradition with their two sons and toast the wing of friendship every time we meet.

> **Let us not take it for granted that life exists more fully in what is commonly thought big than in what is commonly thought small.**
>
> Virginia Woolf (1882–1941)

> **You want to understand always only what you are used to; my mind is reaching out towards things that have never happened.**
>
> *Die Walküre* (1870), Richard Wagner (1813–1883)

My mother was a Wagner fanatic when I was growing up and drummed that one into me!

My favourites for spiritual solace and beautiful words are, in common with many others, I expect:

> **Be joyful, keep the faith and do the little things that you have heard and seen me do.**

St David (500–589), last words to his followers

> **And I said to the man who stood at the gate of the year, 'Give me a light that I may tread safely into the unknown.' And he replied, 'Go out into the darkness and put your hand into the hand of God. That shall be to you better than light and safer than a known way!'**

Minnie Louise Haskins (1875–1957)

# Nigel Seed, judge

I think the quotation that probably serves me most in my life and activity is

**He who hesitates is lost ('Perdition qui haesitat'),**

attributed to Marcus Porcius Cato (234–149 BC), but many say the origin is really unknown.

I consider it not unrelated to Brutus in Shakespeare's *Julius Caesar*:

> **There is a tide in the affairs of men**
> **Which taken at the flood leads on to fortune;**
> **Omitted, all the voyage of their life**
> **Is bound in shallows and in miseries.**
> **On such a full sea we are now afloat,**
> **And we must take the current when it serves,**
> **Or lose our ventures.**
>
> *Julius Caesar* (c. 1599), William Shakespeare (1564–1616)

I would not say I am over-hasty, but I cannot bear dithering or dithered. As a lawyer, of course, I believe all decisions should be reason-based, but the reasoning process should not be unduly prolonged and once a decision has been made, it should be carried out without further debate about the niceties:

**Stand not upon the order of thy going.**

*Macbeth* (c. 1606), William Shakespeare (1564–1616)

Something that I find particularly annoying is when people announce that they are leaving and even go as far as to get up or put on their coats and then initiate new lines of conversation.

A thing that interests me is that people talk too much and listen far too little. I read the obituary of Anthony Cane, chairman of Epsom Downs Racecourse. The last three sentences of his obituary were:

He believed we should listen more than we speak. A lot of us can listen to other people and not hear them. He could.

# Laline Sudlow, graphic designer

**Never say 'no' to adventures. Always say 'yes',
otherwise you'll lead a very dull life.**

Ian Fleming (1908–1964)

———◄◦►———

# Birdy, pop star, composer

I have decided that the best quote of all is:

**Too many cooks spoil the broth.**

My mama has often said this to me and as well as my dinners I've
found that it has applied to many other things in my life, especially in
my music.

# William Ehrman, former chairman of the Joint Intelligence Committee

The one I can think of is from my father, John Ehrman:

**99% of anything achieved in life is down to hard work; 1% is down to talent!**

———◄○►———

# Noel Stewart, milliner

**If you can't love yourself, how the hell are you going to love anybody else?**

RuPaul (born 1960)

**Use your faults, use your defects.**

Édith Piaf (1915–1963)

## Hugh Fearnley-Whittingstall, celebrity chef, writer and campaigner on food and environmental issues

I'd like to offer this from Hippocrates, the father of medicine:

**Let food be your medicine and medicine your food.**

Hippocrates (c. 460–370 BC)

————◄◦►————

## John Bute, former racing driver Johnny Dumfries

I like to keep things simple, so here is a personal motto which has guided me in life:

**Never give up.**

## Rifat Ozbek, Turkish-born designer

**Keep your feet on the ground and your head above the clouds.**

———◄◦►———

## David Fox-Pitt, motivational speaker, author and event manager

**Be ever positive and grateful for all the good things that you have.**

## *Paul Stewart, artist*

There is an Arab proverb that says,

**You don't need to be a chicken to know a good egg**

which stood me in very good stead when I bought my language business, not knowing any myself at all.

**Hope dies last**

used a great deal in Russia.

## Rebecca Fraser, author

**The only thing necessary for the triumph of evil was that good men should do nothing.**

Attributed to Edmund Burke (1729–1797)

---

## Philip Mansel, author and historian

*Il ne faut pas être trop de son pays.*

Isabelle de Charrière (1740–1805).<br>French for 'You shouldn't be too much from where you're from'

Isabelle de Charrière, 1794, exasperated by the conversation of some French émigré refugees.

Or, if you prefer:

*Al galantuomo, ogni paese è patria*

Cardinal Mazarin (1602–1661). Italian for 'A gentleman loves the<br>country where he lives, and loves [cit] it as if it were his native land'

## *Jonathon Porritt, founder and director of Forum for the Future*

I'm offering up one quote from the amazing Thomas Berry:

> **We are not lacking in the dynamic forces needed to create the future. We live immersed in a sea of energy, beyond all comprehension. But this energy, in an ultimate sense, is not ours by domination, but by invocation.**

*Meditations with Thomas Berry* (London: GreenSpirit, 2010), edited by June Raymond

And this is something a little bit more political:

> **Few will have the greatness to bend history itself, but each of us can work to change a small portion of events, and in the total of all those acts will be written the history of this generation.**

Robert Kennedy (1925–1968)

Lastly, one of those quotes from privileged astronauts:

I really believe that if the political leaders of the world could see their planet from a distance of 100,000 miles, their outlook could be fundamentally changed. That all-important border would be invisible, that noisy argument silenced. The tiny globe would continue to turn, serenely ignoring its subdivisions, presenting a unified façade that would cry out for unified understanding. The Earth must become as it appears: blue and white, not capitalist or communist; blue and white, not rich or poor; blue and white, not envious or envied.

*Carrying the Fire: An Astronaut's Journeys* (New York, NY: Farrar, Straus and Giroux, 2009), Michael Collins (born 1930)

# Merlin Erroll, independent crossbench peer

**It is poor civic hygiene to install technologies that could someday facilitate a police state.**

*Secrets and Lies: Digital Security in a Networked World* (Indianapolis IN: Wiley, 2004), Bruce Schneier (born 1963)

**Timid men prefer the calm of despotism to the boisterous sea of liberty.**

Thomas Jefferson (1743–1826)

**Oh judge, your damn laws! The good people don't need them and the bad people don't obey them.**

Ammon Hennacy (1893–1970)

**Everybody blamed Somebody when Nobody did what Anybody could have done.**

Anon.

# Minoo Dinshaw, author

I have decided upon Lord Halifax – not the appeasement one, but the seventeenth-century one, born George Savile. He was a politician more than a philosopher, but certainly something of both and a very wise man indeed. He has a small but very quotable body of work.

> Most men's anger about religion is as if two men should quarrel for a lady they neither of them care for.

> Popularity is a crime from the moment it is sought; it is only a virtue where men have it whether they will or no.

> A man that steps aside from the world, and hath leisure to observe it without interest or design, thinks all mankind as mad as they think him, for not agreeing with them in their mistakes.

> He that leaveth nothing to chance will do few things ill, but he will do very few things.

> Men who borrow their opinions can never repay their debts. They are beggars by nature, and can therefore never get a stock to grow rich upon.

## James Stourton, art historian and former chairman of Sotherby's

*James Stourton has said that he always keeps this in his desk.*

One of the Pharisees invited him to a meal. When he arrived at the Pharisee's house and took his place at table, a women came in, who had a bad name in the town. She had heard he was dining with the Pharisee and had brought with her an alabaster jar of ointment. She waited behind him at his feet, weeping, and her tears fell on his feet, and she wiped them away with her hair; then she covered his feet with kisses and anointed them with the ointment.

When the Pharisee who had invited him saw this, he said to himself, 'If this man were a prophet, he would know who this woman is that is touching him and what a bad name she has.'

Then Jesus took him up and said, 'Simon, I have something to say to you.'

'Speak, Master,' was the reply.

'There was once a creditor who had two men in his debt; one owed him five hundred denarii, the other fifty. They were unable to pay, so he pardoned them both. Which of them will love him more?'

'The one who was pardoned more, I suppose,' answered Simon.

Jesus said, 'You are right.'

Then he turned to the woman. 'Simon,' he said, 'you see this woman? I came into your house, and you poured no water over my feet, but she has poured out her tears over my feet and wiped them away with her hair. You gave me no kiss, but she has been covering my feet with kisses ever since I came in. You did not anoint my head with oil, but she has anointed my feet with ointment. For this reason, I tell you that her sins, her many sins, must have been forgiven her or she would not have shown such great love.'

Luke 7:36–47

49

## Sister Wendy Beckett, religious sister, hermit, art historian

It's always a joy to read St Paul because what he says comes from a very deep understanding of what it means to be baptised. He has grasped to an exceptional degree that baptism is a life-transforming event, and again and again he expresses that in a way that I find unforgettable. Here he is in Galatians 2:20:

**I have been crucified with Christ and I live now not with my own life but with the life of Christ who lives in me.**

Galatians 2:20

That Christ lives in us is the essence of baptism and it affects everything in our lives.

Here is the same deep truth in Colossians 3:3:

**You have died and now the life you have is hidden with Christ in God.**

Colossians 3:3

This of course makes all the difference to our prayer, as Paul says in Romans 8:26:

**The spirit comes to help us in our weakness, for when we cannot choose words in order to pray properly the spirit himself expresses our plea in ways that can never be put into words.**

Romans 8:26

I prefer the old translation, *'sighs too deep for words'*.

But it is not just our prayer that is completely changed by being given to share in the life of God; it affects everything that we do and suffer. In 2 Corinthians 4:8–10 Paul is obviously having a hard time, but he says:

> **We are in difficulties on all sides but never**
> **cornered; we see no answer to our problems, but**
> **never despair; we have been persecuted but never**
> **deserted; knocked down, but never killed; always**
> **wherever we may be, we carry with us in our body**
> **the death of Christ, so that the life of Jesus too,**
> **may always be seen in our body.**

2 Corinthians 4:8–10

*Another quotation that I am especially fond of is also from*
*2 Corinthians. He says that Christ Jesus:*

> **... was never now yes and now no; with Him it**
> **was always yes, and however many the promises**
> **God made the yes to them all is in Him ... He is**
> **our great Amen to the praise of God.**

2 Corinthians 1:18

I love the thought that, though we are unable to respond completely, Jesus within us is always saying yes.

# Father Robin Gibbons, Alexander Schmemann Professor of Eastern Christianity, Eastern Rite Catholic Chaplain for Melkites in the UK, Ecumenical Canon of Christ Church Oxford

Christ is the morning star
who when the night of this world is past
brings to his saints the promise of the light of life
and opens everlasting day.

*Commentary on the Book of Revelation*, Bede (672–735)

The beginning of love is to let those we love be perfectly themselves and not to twist them to fit our own image.

*The Seven Storey Mountain* (San Diego, CA: Harcourt Brace, 1948), Thomas Merton (1915–1968)

God is in the manger, wealth in poverty, light in darkness, succour in abandonment. No evil can befall us; whatever men may do to us, they cannot but serve the God who is secretly revealed as love and rules the world and our lives.

*God Is in the Manger* (Louisville, KY: Westminster John Knox Press, 2010), Dietrich Bonhoeffer (1906–1945)

For the Christian community the Christ event did not change the world but transformed it. In the Risen Christ all things are made new, not abandoned or rejected like rubbish but reformed, recycled so to speak! The ultimate abandonment of death is itself changed and challenged to become for us all, hope in resurrection but also resting in peace.

*For the Life of the World* (Oxford: Peter Lang, 2019), Fr Robin Gibbons

The way to God lies through love of people. At the Last Judgement I shall not be asked whether I was successful in my ascetic exercises, nor how many bows and prostrations I made. Instead I shall be asked: did I feed the hungry, clothe the naked, visit the sick and the prisoners? That is all I shall be asked. About every poor, hungry and imprisoned person the Saviour says 'I': 'I was hungry and thirsty, I was sick and in prison.' To think that he puts an equal sign between himself and anyone in need ... I always knew it, but now it has somehow penetrated to my sinews. It fills me with awe.

Mother Maria of Paris (1891–1945)

Christ in our coming, and in our leaving
the Door and the Keeper,
for us and our dear ones,
this day and every day
blessing for always.
In the name of the Father, the Son and the Holy Spirit. Amen

Blessing for entering and leaving a house, St Brigid of Kildare
(c. 451–525)

You are great, O Lord,
and greatly to be praised;
great is your power,
and your wisdom is infinite.
We would praise you without ceasing.
You call us to delight in your praise,
for you have made us for yourself,
and our hearts find no rest until we rest in you;
with the Father and the Holy Spirit
all glory, praise, and honour be to you,
both now and forevermore. Amen.

Prayer for grace, attributed to St Augustine of Hippo (354–430)

[W]e need to fall, and we need to be aware of it;
for if we did not fall, we should not know how
weak and wretched we are of ourselves, nor
should we know our Maker's marvellous love so
fully ...

*Revelations of Divine Love* (London: Penguin, 1998), Julian of Norwich
(c. 1342–1416), translated by Elizabeth Spearing

God, of your goodness, give me Yourself;
for You are enough for me,
and I can ask for nothing less
that can be full honour to You.
And if I ask anything that is less,
ever shall I be in want,
for only in You have I all.

Prayer, Julian of Norwich (c. 1342–1416)

... the Rood of the Lord,
that I espied here upon the earth,
shall ferry me from this loaned life
and bring me then where there is great bliss,
joys in heaven, where there are the people of the
   Lord,
seated at the feast, where there is everlasting
   happiness
and seat me where I will be allowed afterwards
to dwell in glory, brooking joys well amid the
   sainted.
May the Lord be my friend, who suffered before
here on earth, on the gallows-tree for the sins of
   man

'The Dream of the Rood' (accessed 15/04/19 from
anglosaxonpoetry.camden.rutgers.edu/dream-of-the-rood),
translated by Dr Aaron K Hostetter

By a Carpenter mankind was made, and only by
that Carpenter can mankind be remade.

Desiderius Erasmus (1466–1536)

Like a bee one should extract from each of the
virtues what is most profitable. In this way, by
taking a small amount from all of them, one builds
up from the practice of the virtues a great
honeycomb overflowing with the soul-delighting
honey of wisdom.

*The Philokalia*, vol. IV (London: Faber and Faber, 1995), St Gregory of
Sinai (c. 1260–1346), translated by G E H Palmer,
Philip Sherrard and Kallistos Ware

# Nigel Thomas, barrister and part-time judge

I have chosen the prayer of St Richard of Chichester, who died in 1253; supposedly it was composed on his deathbed. About twenty years ago I worked on a long case in Chichester and took the opportunity of going to cathedral evensong from time to time. On one such occasion I found a prayer card which contained this touching little prayer. I kept the card in my wallet until alas the wallet was stolen.

> **Thanks be to Thee, my Lord Jesus Christ,**
> **For all the benefits you have given me,**
> **O most merciful Redeemer, friend and brother,**
> **May I know You more clearly,**
> **Love You more dearly,**
> **Follow You more nearly.**

St Richard of Chichester (1197–1253)

———◄○►———

# Caroline Blunden, Chinese painting consultant, author and artist

> **More things are wrought by prayer than this world dreams of.**

Alfred, Lord Tennyson (1809–1892)

## Jane Blunden, author of the Bradt travel guide to Mongolia

*Jane Blunden helped a group of zoo breeders to return the wild horses to Mongolia: 'that great little tough pony that survives today in Mongolia despite all the odds.'*

As it's Pentecost Sunday, I'd like to send you a family verse that my father used frequently.

**In all things God works for the good of those who love him.**

Romans 8:28

**And from memory the older version he so often used (especially when things weren't working out well!) was *'All things work together for the good …'***

**It certainly encouraged us all!**

## Liz Fenwick, author

The first thing that came to my mind was a prayer written by Thomas Merton. It was the one thing that brought me through my turbulent late teens and twenties. I recently came upon it again (funny how it appeared again when I needed it) and I find it still gives me solace when my life is on an uncertain path.

**My Lord God,**
**I have no idea where I am going.**

**I do not see the road ahead of me.**

**I cannot know for certain where it will end. Nor do I really know myself, and the fact that I think that I am following your will does not mean that I am actually doing so.**

**But I believe that the desire to please you does in fact please you. And I hope I have that desire in all that I am doing. I hope that I will never do anything apart from that desire. And I know that if I do this, you will lead me by the right road though I may know nothing about it.**

**Therefore will I trust you always though I may seem to be lost and in the shadow of death. I will not fear, for you are ever with me, and you will never leave me to face my perils alone.**

**Amen.**

Thomas Merton (1915–1968)

## Melanie McDonough, journalist

What lifts me up most when I have made a mess of things is Christ's words, in Revelation, as the King who sits on the throne.

**Behold, I make all things new.**

Revelation 21:5

So, we are not always bound by our mistakes and stupidity in the past but can start things all over again. And what could be better?

# Frances Rattray, lawyer

Here is a modest contribution for your collection:

**The glory of God is a man fully alive.**

St Irenaeus of Lyons (130–202)

The text that I have always found profoundly inspiring is a sermon by Metropolitan Anthony Bloom:

> **In the gospels we read that death is at our elbow, that much, very much, of what we do will perish with us as unnecessary, mortal.**

> **Does this mean that Christ's warning about the closeness of death should frighten us and deprive us of creative strength? No, on the contrary; the Fathers used to say, 'keep a constant memory of death,' not in the sense that we should be afraid of death and live under its constant shadow, but rather because nothing but the awareness of the fact that life is short, that it may end at any moment, can give to every moment its final meaning, and to the whole of life the feeling that we must hurry to do good, that we must hurry to live in such a way that at whatever moment death overtakes us, it will be a moment of triumphant life. We would live with such depth, so intensely, if only this awareness were with us constantly. If we were to know that the words that I am now speaking to you were the last, how differently would I say them, and how differently would you listen!**

If we were to feel that the person we were talking to might be dead within a few minutes, how careful we should be that our words and actions in relation to him should be the culmination of all the love and care of which we are capable, that they should be the triumph of everything that is best and highest in our relationship.

The reason that we live so badly, utter so many empty words, rotten words, dead words, commit so many actions that afterwards burn in our soul like wounds, is that we live as though this life was merely a rough draft of the life we will one day be living, when we have had time to shape the draft into the final story. But that is not how things work; death comes and the draft remains rough, his life has not been lived, just blotted, and there remains regret for the person who could have been great, but turned out shallow and insignificant.

That is what today's Gospel is about, not that we should be afraid of death, but that, knowing that it can come at any moment, every moment must be perfect, every word must be a word of life, filled with the Spirit, fit to enter eternity. And every action of ours in relation to each one of us should be such as to give life and express the fullness and depth and strength of the love and reverence which we should feel for each other and for all. Let us consider this, and then if we can act upon it, every word and every action will acquire the dimension of eternity and shine with its light. Amen.

Metropolitan Anthony of Sourozh (1914–2003)

# Father Joseph Campo, priest

**Everything is grace.**

St Thérèse of Lisieux (1873–1897)

This extended the meaning of grace to unprecedented and all-encompassing proportions and gave a decided lustre to the term.

**I am not dying but entering life.**

St Thérèse of Lisieux (1873–1897)

**I will let fall from heaven a shower of roses.**

St Thérèse of Lisieux (1873–1897)

The quotes are so beautiful from Thérèse, the greatest saint of modern times, as she was called by Pius X if I recall correctly. He also adopted her as his second guardian angel.

# Janet Scrymgeour Wedderburn, sculptor and painter

God speaks in a still small voice to the soul, so
small that any noise of creatures can distract
from it.

*Silent creaturae, silentium est Christus.*

Martin D'Arcy SJ (1887–1976). Latin for 'Let creatures be still, for the
silence is Christ'

Silence is a sea,
while the stream is busy chatter.
The sea will find you,
but you must first arise from the stream.

Jalal ad-Din Muhammad Rumi (1207–1273)

When love strikes, nothing can help the love-struck
but love.

Jalal ad-Din Muhammad Rumi (1207–1273)

*Volé tan alto, tan alto
Que di a la caza alcance.*

St John of the Cross (1542–1591).
Spanish for 'I flew so high, so high that I reached my quarry'

(The lover on his flight to union with God is compared to a falcon
that flies so high and then swoops.)

Do not be fearful of death.
Welcome it when it comes.
It is now a holy thing,
made so by him who died that we might live.

Basil Hume (1923–1999)

Oh Christ my Lord. I pray that you will turn my heart to you in the depth of my being, where with the noise of creatures silenced and the clamour of bothersome thoughts stilled, I shall stay with you where I find you always present.

Leonardus Lessius (1554–1623)

Lord, where shall I find you?
High and hidden is your place.
And where shall I not find you?
The world is full of your glory.
I have sought your nearness,
With all my heart I called you
And in going out to meet you
I found you coming in to meet me.

Judah Halevi (c. 1075 – 1141)

You who are love itself give me the grace of love, give me yourself,
so that all my days may finally empty into the one day of your eternal life.

Karl Rahner (1904–1984)

———◄○►———

# William Roper-Curzon, artist

E'en eternity's too short to extol thee.

Hymn, George Herbert (1593–1633)

# Nick Pearson, psychotherapist

We empty our hearts of reflective thinking, and we sit together with God on the carpet of tact and spiritual attentiveness and presence and readiness to receive *whatever* comes to us from Him – so that it is God who takes care of teaching us by means of unveiling and spiritual realisation. Once they have this inner receptivity, God manifests Himself to them, teaching them and informing them through the direct inner vision.

Ibn Arabi (1165–1240)

The evil we are suffering from is less a split between Faith and Reason than between Reason and an Imagination that has become incapable of linking the two parts of the Universe, the Visible and the Invisible.

Carl Jung (1875–1961)

Ah thou Beauty,
So ancient and so fresh,
Too late have I come to know thee,
For behold, thou wert inside
And I out of myself
Where I made search for thee.

St Augustine (354–430)

Dissatisfaction is the greatest curse,
to be ungrateful even worse,
and even worse than this
to chase illusions and then miss,
the great dis-ease we cast
around our Selves.
Listen, Friend,
just learn to sit,
and with your heart
consider Gratefulness.
Maybe learn to thank the stars
you have a roof, no prison bars
and bread.
And look, there's sunlight on the wall,
and even in the storm-cloud's pall
lineaments of Beauty.

'Gratefulness', Nick Pearson

Today, like every other day, we awake empty
And frightened. Don't open the door to the study
And begin reading.
Let the beauty we love be what we do.
There are hundreds of ways to kneel and kiss the
ground.

Jalal ad-Din Muhammad Rumi (1207–1273)

## John Jolliffe, author

In the hour of my distress,
When temptations me oppress,
And when I my sins confess,
Sweet Spirit comfort me!

When I lie within my bed,
Sick in heart
And sick in head,
And with doubts discomforted,
Sweet Spirit comfort me!

When the house doth sigh and weep,
And the world is drown'd in sleep,
Yet mine eyes the watch do keep,
Sweet Spirit comfort me!

When (God knows) I'm tossed about,
Either with despair or doubt,
Yet before the glass be out,
Sweet Spirit comfort me!

When the judgement is reveal'd
And that open'd which was seal'd,
When to Thee I have appeal'd,
Sweet Spirit comfort me!

Robert Herrick (1591–1674)

O Christ, a light transcendent
Shines in Thy countenance
And none can tell the sweetness,
The beauty of Thy glance.
In this may Thy poor servants
Their joy eternal find;
Thou calledst them; O rest them,
Thou lover of mankind.

St John Damascene (676–749)


Preserve my soul, O Lord, because it belongs to
Thee, and preserve my body because it belongs to
my soul. Thou alone dost steer my boat through all
its voyage, but hast a more especial care of it,
when it comes to a narrow current, or to a
dangerous fall of waters. Thou hast a care of the
preservation of my body in all the ways of my life;
but, in the straits of death, open Thine eyes wider,
and enlarge Thy providence towards me so far that
no illness or agony may shake and benumb the
soul. Do Thou so make my bed in all my sickness
that, being used to Thy hand, I may be content with
any bed of Thy making.

John Donne (1572–1631)

# Sebastian Brock, academic and Syriac expert

What watering is to plants is exactly the same as continual silence for the growth of spiritual knowledge.

St Isaac the Syrian (640–880)

In love did God bring the world into existence; in love does He guide it during its temporal existence; in love is He going to bring it to that wondrous transformed state, and in love will the world be swallowed up in the great mystery of Him who has performed all these things. In love will the whole cause of the governance of creation be finally comprised.

St Isaac the Syrian (640–880)

Just because the terms 'wrath', 'anger', 'hatred' and the rest are used of the creator in the Bible, we should not imagine that He actually does anything in anger, hatred or zeal. Many figurative terms are used of God in the scriptures, terms which are far removed from His true nature.

St Isaac the Syrian (640–880)

## Stefan Reynolds, author, teacher at Christian Meditation Centre

It seems to me that the person who is about to come to prayer should withdraw for a little and prepare themselves, and so become more attentive and active for the whole of their prayer ... They should cast away all temptation and troubling thoughts and should put away all extraneous things. This is how they should come to prayer, stretching out their soul, as it were, instead of their hands, straining their mind towards God instead of their eyes. All malice towards any one of those who seem to have wronged them should be put away ... Now concerning the place, let it be known that every place is suitable for prayer if a person prays well ... But everyone may have, if I may put it this way, a holy place set aside and chosen in their own house, if possible, for accomplishing their prayers in quiet and without distraction.

Origen (184–253)

# Rodney Thompson, hermit

*A former Benedictine monk, Rodney Thompson has been a hermit in Connemara (without running water or electricity) since the mid-1980s, under the Archbishop of Tuam.*

One of the desert Fathers, Arsenius, said, 'Flee, be silent, pray always.'

We will consider each of these in turn, starting off with solitude.

## Solitude

We enter into solitude 'to be with Our Lord and with Him alone, to dwell in the gentle healing presence of Our Lord.' He is the Love of our Life. He is beside us in all that we do, inspiring our thoughts and impulses, guiding our footsteps. Abba Elias said that he heard a voice which said to him, 'As soon as you turned to me, I was beside you.' We also go into solitude to discover our true selves. Thomas Merton said that the desert fathers had come into the desert to be themselves and that they insisted on remaining human and ordinary. When we are living in society, it is often difficult to resist the pressure to be what other people want us to be. We try to live up to their expectations of us. We often develop a false sense, a persona, to cope with living in the world among other people. But in solitude, with God's help, we gradually get rid of our scaffolding; our false self disappears and we discover our true self. The great discovery we make, which sets us free, is that God loves us just as we are with all our strengths and weaknesses.

'I have loved you with an everlasting love; I am constant in my affection for you.' (Jer 31:2–4)

We also learn to simplify our lives so that our sense of self does not depend upon what we possess or what we plan (status, qualifications, etc.). As St Francis said, 'I am what I am in God's eyes, no more and no less.' Poverty, as I understand it, is to try to need less rather than want more, to try and simplify our lives.

But I don't want to suggest for one moment that the desert fathers and hermits turn their back on people. St Anthony the Great, regarded as the father of the desert monks, took his solitude with him wherever he went, after he had spent twenty years in the desert. His solitude was a quality of his heart. After all his struggles and purification alone in the desert, his life was transformed and he had become a really compassionate human being. He had an extraordinary effect upon people who met him. They felt healed just by seeing him, he was fitted with such a quality of peace and harmony. One visitor said, 'It is enough for me to see you, Father.'

Compassion is the fruit of solitude. We suffer with our brothers and sisters. We enter into solidarity with them. We give up measuring our meaning and value in relation to others. We become non-judgemental. We stop forcing people to live up to our judgements of them. Many stories from the desert bear witness to this compassion. 'Do not have hostile feelings towards anyone'; 'Do not let

dislike of anyone dominate your life.' Real
forgiveness becomes possible. There is a lovely story
told about Abba Moses, who was asked to come and
judge a disobedient hermit. So he came trailing a
leaking jug behind him and said nothing. When
asked what was the meaning of this, he replied, 'My
sins run out behind me and I do not see them, and
you ask me to come and judge another!' A
compassionate person is so aware of the suffering of
another that he is not aware of their sins. He has
also come to know himself that he is wary of
judging others.


## Silence

Silence is the way to make solitude a reality. The
hermitage is properly a place where the whole life is
brought back to listening to God. Fragility, solitude
and other monastic disciplines are all directed to
this end. And yet a hermit can go to considerable
trouble and put up with a lot of discomfort to live in
external solitude and spoil the whole purpose of his
life by too much 'noise', e.g. having his radio turned
on a lot of the time. This is often to mitigate the
loneliness that he feels. The sound of human voice
can be very comforting to one who lives alone.

Of course it is necessary for hermits to relax at
times and listen to music, tapes and the radio, and
also to show hospitality to visitors. But how right St
Benedict is to emphasise the great value of silence
from monks. Silence guards the life of the Holy

Spirit within, which is compared to a fire within us, which we must tend. Steam loses its heat if the doors are left open in a steam bath. We should have a tendency to silence at all times, even with visitors, and then we might have something really worthwhile or helpful to say. Alas, so often the door of our steam bath is left open, the words pour out and we quench the fire of God's Spirit within us. We don't trust the Spirit within us to touch people's hearts. One of the desert fathers said ... 'I have often repented of having spoken but never of being silent.' All the desert fathers are in agreement that charity, not silence, is the purpose of the Spiritual Life.

## Prayer

If silence is the way to make solitude a reality, unceasing prayer is the way to make our silence fruitful. The desert fathers do not offer any theory about prayer, but their wonderful stories and wise sayings were the stones used by later writers to develop their 'prayer of the heart', 'prayer of rest, the soul at rest in God'. Isaac the Syrian said that the way to God is through 'the heart'. The heart here refers to the source of our emotional and volitional (i.e. of the will) perception, the very centre or deepest centre of the person. Heart and Will are synonymous. Some desert fathers describe prayer as 'the mind descending into the heart'. Macarius the Great says, 'The chief task of the monk is to enter into the heart. Let his prayer re-model his whole person.' Unless we are praying with the heart, our vocal prayers are mere words and our meditation is little more than a philosophical contemplation of God.

But how are we to fix our hearts on God so that we are 'praying without ceasing' as St Paul commands us to do? We need to use *key words,* such as 'Love', 'Abba, Father' or the *Jesus Prayer:* 'Lord Jesus Christ, have mercy on me, a sinner' – which I also find very helpful and use a lot. In that beautiful book *The Way of a Pilgrim* a holy *staretz* (spiritual father) teaches a Russian peasant who is very anxious to fulfil St Paul's command to pray without ceasing the Jesus Prayer. The prayer becomes his true companion on his journey. At first it was a great struggle and effort, but eventually the prayer took over inside him even while he was engaged in manual work or talking to others. The Holy Spirit comes to help us in our weakness when we cannot pray properly, and eventually we find it becomes much less of an effort until we enter the prayer of rest, the soul rest in God at all times. I would strongly recommend that in a real crisis, e.g. trapped in an earthquake, underground train etc., keep repeating the Jesus Prayer. It will calm you.

'Desert Spirituality', talk given in Barna (8 July 2011),
Rodney Thompson

## Kenneth Thompson, sculptor

The night has a thousand eyes,
And the day but one;
Yet the light of the bright world dies
With the dying sun.
The mind has a thousand eyes,
And the heart but one;
Yet the light of a whole life dies
When love is done.

'Light', Francis William Bourdillon (1852–1921)

Only a sweet and virtuous soul,
Like season'd timber, never gives;
But though the whole world turn to coal,
Then chiefly lives.

George Herbert (1593–1633)

To see a World in a Grain of Sand
And a Heaven in a Wild Flower
Hold Infinity in the palm of your hand
And Eternity in an hour

'Auguries of Innocence', William Blake (1757–1827)

He who binds to himself a joy
Does the wingéd life destroy
But he who kisses the joy as it flies
Lives in eternity's sunrise

'Eternity', William Blake (1757–1827)

Similar to Blake's poem, which was the first inscription I carved in stone in Liverpool in 1969:

**Joy & Woe are woven fine, a clothing for the soul Divine.**

## Antony Sutch, educationalist

Though truth and falsehood be
Near twins, yet Truth a little elder is.
Be busy to seek her; believe me this:
He's not of none, nor worst, that seeks the best

John Donne (1572–1631)

I wake and feel the fell of dark, not day.
What hours, O what black hours we have spent
This night! What sights you, heart, saw, ways you went!
And more must, in yet longer light's delay.

Gerald Manley Hopkins (1844–1889)

It is almost a dark night of the soul, of life itself – based on the self-centredness of ego.

## Lettice Buxton, lay minister

A noiseless patient spider,
I marked where on a little promontory it stood isolated,
Mark'd how to explore the vacant vast surrounding,
It launch'd forth filament, filament, filament, out of itself,
Ever unreeling them, ever tirelessly speeding them.

And you O my soul where you stand,
Surrounded, detached, in measureless oceans of space,
Ceaselessly musing, venturing, throwing, seeking the
   spheres to connect them,
Till the bridge you will need be form'd, till the ductile
   anchor hold,
Till the gossamer thread you fling catch somewhere, O my
   soul.

'A Noiseless Patient Spider', Walt Whitman (1819–1892)

# *Antonia Fraser, author, writer of history*

What sound was that?

I turn away, into the shaking room.

What was that sound that came in on the dark?
What is this maze of light it leaves us in?
What is this stance we take,
To turn away and then turn back?
What did we hear?

It was the breath we took when we first met.

Listen. It is here.

'It Is Here', Harold Pinter (1930–2008)
Published by Faber and Faber

# Ian A Olson, doctor, historian and poet

From *Facing the Persians:*

> In the trees above me
> The blackbird sings
> As I sit here at my table
> With my books and my writing things.
>
> A cuckoo cries out to me
> From his bush, with a grey hood.
> Oh, dear God, how happy I am,
> Writing here, under the great wood.

'The Scribe Under the Trees', Ian A Olson

After lines written by a diverted Irish monk of the ninth century. They were inscribed in the margin of a manuscript he was meant to be copying. *'How cared for, how looked after I am'* comes nearer to the original Irish.

> When grey shapes slip the shadows of the morning
> My small birds sit in silence in the eaves ...
>
> Their end is woven into their existence
> Their deaths a fitness that their fate contrives
> But here a helpless watcher from the window
> Can scarce accept the lesson of their lives

'When Grey Shapes Slip the Shadows', Ian A Olson

## Candia McWilliam, author

I'm doing a sort of sortes Vergilianae and LEAPING. As a small child of four or five, I was taught this round that hasn't left my head.

*Pauper sum ego.*
*Nihil habeo.*
*Cor meum dabo.*

Latin for 'I am poor. I have nothing. You have my heart'

Here is this beautiful song about Mary:

I sing of a maiden
That is makeles,
King of all kings
To her sone sche ches.

He cam also stille
There his moder was,
As dew in Aprille
That falleth on the grass.

He cam also stille
To his moderes bour,
As dew in Aprille
That falleth on the flour.

He cam also stille
There his moder lay,
As dew in Aprille
That falleth on the spray.

Moder and maiden
Was never non but sche;
Well may swich a lady
Godes moder be

'I Sing of a Maiden', traditional song

This has something strongly of the spirit, and of the spirit of a child; and of a Scottish childhood, I think?

As from the house your mother sees
You playing round the garden trees,
So you may see, if you will look
Through the windows of this book,
Another child, far, far away,
And in another garden, play.
But do not think you can at all,
By knocking on the window, call
That child to hear you. He intent
Is all on his play-business bent.
He does not hear; he will not look,
Nor yet be lured out of this book.
For, long ago, the truth to say,
He has grown up and gone away,
And it is but a child of air
That lingers in the garden there.

'To Any Reader', Robert Louis Stevenson (1850–1894)

Hard to choose from this poet who is so dear to me.

I made a posy, while the day ran by:
'Here will I smell my remnant out, and tie
My life within this band.'
But Time did beckon to the flowers, and they
By noon most cunningly did steal away,
And withered in my hand.

My hand was next to them, and then my heart;
I took, without more thinking, in good part
Time's gentle admonition;
Who did so sweetly death's sad taste convey,
Making my mind to smell my fatal day,
Yet, sug'ring the suspicion.

Farewell dear flowers, sweetly your time ye spent,
Fit, while ye lived, for smell or ornament,
And after death for cures.
I follow straight without complaints or grief,
Since, if my scent be good, I care not if
It be as short as yours.

'Life', George Herbert (1593–1633)

Lord, how can man preach thy eternal word?
He is a brittle crazy glass;
Yet in thy temple thou dost him afford
This glorious and transcendent place,
To be a window, through thy grace.

But when thou dost anneal in glass thy story,
Making thy life to shine within
The holy preachers, then the light and glory
More reverend grows, and more doth win;
Which else shows waterish, bleak, and thin.

Doctrine and life, colours and light, in one
When they combine and mingle, bring
A strong regard and awe; but speech alone
Doth vanish like a flaring thing,
And in the ear, not conscience, ring.

'The Windows', George Herbert (1593–1633)

I think that the great passage from Proust where the narrator sees the books of the dead great novelist Bergotte in a shop window by night is deeply relevant.

The circumstances of his death were as follows. A fairly mild attack of uraemia had led to his being ordered to rest. But, an art critic having written somewhere that in Vermeer's 'View of Delft' (lent by the Gallery at The Hague for an exhibition of Dutch painting), a picture which he adored and imagined that he knew by heart, a little patch of yellow wall (which he could not remember) was so well painted that it was, if one looked at it by itself, like some priceless specimen of Chinese art, of a beauty that was sufficient in itself, Bergotte ate a few potatoes, left the house, and went to the exhibition. At the first few steps he had to climb, he was overcome by an attack of dizziness. He walked past several pictures and was struck by the aridity and pointlessness of such an artificial kind of art, which was greatly inferior to the sunshine of a windswept Venetian palazzo, or of an ordinary house by the sea. At last he came to the Vermeer which he remembered as more striking, more different from anything else he knew, but in which, thanks to the critic's article, he noticed for the first time some small figures in blue, that the sand was pink, and, finally, the precious substance of the tiny patch of yellow wall. His dizziness increased; he fixed his gaze, like a child upon a yellow butterfly that it wants to catch, on the precious little patch of wall. 'That's how I ought to have written,' he said. 'My last books are too dry, I ought to have gone over them with a few layers of colour, made my language precious in itself, like this little patch of yellow wall.' Meanwhile he was not unconscious of the gravity of his condition. In a celestial pair of scales there appeared to him, weighing down one the pans, his own life, while the other contained the little patch of wall so beautifully painted in yellow. He felt that he had rashly sacrificed the former for the latter. 'All the same,' he said to himself, 'I shouldn't like to be the headline news of this exhibition for the evening papers.' He repeated to himself: 'Little patch of yellow wall, with a sloping roof, little patch of yellow wall.' Meanwhile he sank down on to a circular settee; whereupon he suddenly ceased to think that his life was in jeopardy and, reverting to his natural optimism, told himself: 'It's nothing, merely a touch of indigestion from those potatoes, which were undercooked.' A fresh attack struck him down; he rolled from the settee to the floor, as visitors and attendants came hurrying to his assistance. He was dead. Dead for ever? Who can say? Certainly, experiments in spiritualism offer us no more proof than the dogmas of religion that the soul survives death. All that we can say is that everything is arranged in this life as though we entered it carrying a burden of obligations contracted in a former life; there is no reason inherent in the conditions of life on this earth that can make us consider ourselves obliged to do good, to be kind and thoughtful, even to be polite, nor for an atheist artist to consider himself obliged to begin over again a score of times a piece of work the admiration aroused by which will matter little to his worm-eaten body, like the patch of yellow wall painted with so much skill and refinement by an artist destined to be forever unknown and barely identified under the name Vermeer. All these obligations, which have no sanction in our present life, seem to belong to a different world, a world based on kindness, scrupulousness, self-sacrifice, a world entirely different from this one and which we leave in order to be born on this earth, before perhaps returning there to live once again beneath sway of those unknown laws which we obeyed because we bore their precepts in our hearts, not knowing whose hand had traced them there – those laws to which every profound work of the intellect brings us nearer and which are invisible only – if then! – to fools. So that the idea that Bergotte was not dead for ever is by no means improbable.

They buried him, but all through that night of mourning, in the lighted shop-windows, his books, arranged three by three, kept vigil like angels with outspread wings and seemed, for him who was no more, the symbol of his resurrection.

*The Captive* (London: Chatto & Windus, 1951), Marcel Proust (1871–1922), translated by C K Scott Moncrieff